Old OLLERTON

by
David Ottewell

CW00959247

A view of Ollerton post office dating from prior to 1905. Originally the post office was situated in the Hop Pole Hotel and catered for all the local villages including Edwinstowe. Later it moved into the premises seen here. These had been built as a farmhouse in Georgian times and were later adapted to house a chemists. In Kelly's Directory for 1908 Arthur Morris is listed as both chemist and postmaster.

© David Ottewell 2002
First published in the United Kingdom, 2002,
by Stenlake Publishing
Telephone / Fax: 01290 551122

ISBN 1 84033 203 4

THE PUBLISHERS REGRET THAT THEY CANNOT SUPPLY
COPIES OF ANY PICTURES FEATURED IN THIS BOOK.

FURTHER READING

The books listed below were used by the author during his research. None of them are available from Stenlake Publishing. Those interested in finding out more are advised to contact their local bookshop or reference library.

R. Adam, ed., *So This Was Ollerton*, 1986
D. J. Bradbury, *Ollerton BC*, Wheel Publications, 1985
T. Breeze, ed., *Village Voices; Ollerton After the Pit*, 1995
J. B. Firth, *Highways and Byways in Nottinghamshire*, 1924
C. Gibson et al., *Our Ollerton*

The *Worksop Guardian* of 29 April 1932 described Ollerton thus: 'Viewed from a distance Ollerton, with its church tower, its old mill, the long red brick front of the Hop Pole Hotel and the deeper red brick of the hall, presents a charming and picturesque appearance, and though there may be some little disillusionment, as one enters the narrow streets of this quaint old world little town, the visitor will find much to interest him and an unfailing source of enjoyment in the delightful wooded scenery close at hand.'

Opposite: The River Maun rises near Annesley and at Fountaindale and flows via Mansfield and Edwinstowe to join the River Idle. The settlement of Ollerton grew up close by the point where the Maun and the smaller Rainworth Water converge. The river provided power for milling and a watermill still operates in Ollerton today. The great flood of 1795 destroyed the bridge over the river.

INTRODUCTION

Ollerton is situated amidst beautiful countryside on the eastern edge of Sherwood Forest. The village covered an area of approximately 1,700 acres before its expansion in the twentieth century.

The settlement known today as Ollerton grew initially because of the joining of two water courses; the River Maun and the Rainworth Water. These met in a clearing of Sherwood Forest. The date of the first settlers in the area is unknown, but the thickness of the forest and its inhospitable nature discouraged the Romans so it is believed that it was Anglo–Saxon times before a settlement was established.

The first name associated with the area is Allerton or Alretun by which the village is referred to in the Domesday Book. It means 'the farm of the alders'. In the Domesday Book Alretun was recorded as being divided into two manors; one owned by Gilbert de Gand, a nephew of William the Conqueror, and the other by Roger de Busli, who at the time of the Conquest became the main landowner in Nottinghamshire.

In the twelfth century a group of Cistercians built Rufford Abbey near the village, probably in part attracted by the three watermills in operation in the area. They requisitioned one of these mills for their own use.

By the first quarter of the thirteenth century Ollerton had a church with its own priest, although this situation was short-lived as before the end of the century it was taken over and put under the control of the priest at Edwinstowe. However, Ollerton did have some influence in local affairs

for it was a meeting place for forest officials, while local courts were also conducted there. From the early seventeenth century until the 1930s much of Ollerton and the surrounding area was owned by the Savile family, who were based at Rufford Abbey, about a mile south of the village.

Ollerton was a largely rural settlement, its Enclosure Act being passed in 1768. However, its situation at the junction of the main north–south (from Doncaster to Leicester) and east–west (from Newark to Sheffield) roads had a big influence on its development. Roads brought trade, even if only of the passing sort. Up until the eighteenth century highwaymen were at work in the area so a safe haven to stop, take refreshment and change horses was invaluable. Both the White Hart and the Hop Pole catered for travellers.

At the start of the nineteenth century Ollerton was still basically a small rural community with a population of just 439. By 1830 the total had only risen to 658, and these inhabitants were concentrated in 130 dwellings. The chief crops grown were wheat, barley, oats and roots. Up until the nineteenth century Ollerton had also been a major hop growing area, and a survey of 1798 found 30 acres of hops there. At this time Ollerton was one of ten market towns in Nottinghamshire holding a small market each Friday. It also had two annual fairs, one on May Day and the other in October to coincide with the hop harvest. Ollerton was not officially declared a town until 1993 when the town hall was opened.

The nineteenth century saw the beginning of the development of an area to the north-east of the village which was given the name New Ollerton. Initially this covered only a small patch of land stretching from where the police station is today to the Plough Inn.

A major change in Ollerton's fortunes occurred in the 1920s when exploration for coal by the Butterley Company proved that there were large, accessible reserves locally that it would be economic to mine. The company invested not only in Ollerton Colliery but also in a community of approximately 1,000 houses and associated buildings including shops, churches and centres of entertainment. Miners and their families were attracted not only from the rest of the county but in large numbers from the north-east and Scotland. By 1931 there were 3,912 people living in Ollerton.

Other changes took place between the world wars: the Savile estate was broken up and many of the buildings in Ollerton were sold at auction. The most significant recent change in the life of Ollerton and its people was the closure of the colliery in the 1990s. Locals are still coming to terms as to the implications of this for the future.

E.L.S. 235-11. Ollerton.

Although the water power of the River Maun was potentially useful, and was harnessed to drive the water wheel at the mill (seen to the far right of this picture), it could also prove destructive. There were a number of floods with particularly bad ones occurring in 1795, 1921 and 1931. There has been a mill on this site for at least 700 years, although the present structure dates from the eighteenth century. For many years it has been in the hands of the Mettam family. This open view in front of the Hop Pole is somewhat different from today, with a car park now occupying the grassy area in the foreground.

4

Ollerton Hall can trace its origins to the seventeenth century, although it stands on the site of an even earlier manor house. It is thought to have been built by Thomas Markham, the most famous member of whose family was Colonel George Markham. He fought for the Royalist cause in the Civil War and was killed at Gainsborough, after which his body was brought back to Ollerton for burial. Later the hall passed to the ownership of the Saviles of Rufford. *Black's Guide to Nottinghamshire* (1887) describes the hall as: 'a venerable brick and stone mansion . . . having a fine doorway and spacious entrance hall with a large and handsome stairway leading to the apartments on the upper storey'. In the 1920s the Butterley Colliery Company took the hall over when developing Ollerton Colliery. Plans were made for it to become a charity-run nursing home in the 1990s, but these did not come to fruition and sadly over the last decade it has been allowed to badly deteriorate.

Like all communities that had lost men in the First World War, Ollerton decided to erect a memorial to its dead. The site chosen was a triangular piece of land by the River Maun which was donated by Lord Savile of Rufford Abbey. Public subscriptions raised £200 and a memorial, made out of Hopton stone, was unveiled in 1919. It bore sixteen names. Ollerton was affected even more directly by the Second World War. A pair of 500 lb bombs landed near New Ollerton but luckily neither exploded and both were eventually successfully defused. A number of American soldiers were based at the nearby Proteus and Boughton camps. Ollerton also played host to evacuees from London and of course Bevan boys were sent to work in the pit.

The building to the left is Forest House, a red-brick Georgian farmhouse. It served its original purpose into the twentieth century and in 1908 John Charles Wood, farmer, is recorded as living there. By 1925 ownership had transferred to a Mr Ward, also a farmer, although by 1936 Mrs E. Ward (possibly his wife) is listed as the proprietor of a hotel at the same address. The development of tourism probably resulted in this change of use, and today the premises remain an inn, although the name has been changed.

Estate cottages at Forest Corner. A number of sporting events such as football and cricket matches took place on the open ground around here during the early years of the twentieth century. The main road bypassing the village was taken along this route in 1925.

A 1920s picture of Forest Corner. Even at this time it was an important traffic junction, being the place where the Nottingham to Doncaster road intersected with the east–west road. Note the large number of telegraph poles stretching into the village.

The same junction about thirty years later. As the place where six roads meet, it had been tidied up with a roundabout by this point.

E.L.S. 235-1. Ollerton.

Coming into Ollerton over the River Maun via the humpback bridge opens up this vista. Mettam's watermill has just been passed on the right, while the lad posing between the shafts of the horseless cart is outside George Essam's butchers shop. In the 1908 directory George's wife is listed as carrying on the trade of photographer; an important service to the village at a time when few households owned their own camera.

On crossing the Maun into Ollerton village, the visitor was immediately confronted by a choice of two establishments offering refreshments: the Hop Pole Hotel to the left and the Sherwood Café to the right. The prime position of this pair is likely to have given them the edge over much of the competition for customers in the village. Although the roads are empty of traffic on this postcard, this was the inter-war period which saw an upsurge in private car ownership and hence travel for pleasure.

Ollerton Church.

Rex Series 762.

The first mention of a church in Ollerton dates from around AD 1200, although this was soon subsumed into the parish of Edwinstowe. The vicar of Edwinstowe thus had pastoral care not only for his own village but for the neighbouring settlements of Ollerton, Clipstone, Budby, Carburton and Perlethorpe. In 1777 the original church was in an extremely run-down state and the present building was erected in its place. This was in turn restored in 1860 providing seating for 280 worshippers. It was not until 1888 that Ollerton became a separate parish again, the first vicar being Revd John William Paley Reade.

Ollerton Church, situated as it is in Sherwood Forest, is appropriately dedicated to St Giles, a seventh century Athenian hermit who resided in a French forest. In his *Highways and Byways of Nottinghamshire*, J. B. Frith is very dismissive of Ollerton church, referring to it as 'a poor structure both without and within. The battlemented tower is both squat and clumsy.' It is true that it is somewhat unprepossessing when compared with some of Nottinghamshire's other churches. The tower contains seven bells of which six were presented by Cecil George Savile Foljambe in 1875, the same year that the clock was paid for by public subscription. The same Mr Foljambe, who resided at Cockglode House (see page 48), also arranged for the coloured east window to be fitted in 1873 as a memorial to his first wife, Louisa Blanche. A window on the south side is dedicated to Mrs Lumley Savile.

The Post Office, Ollerton.

A springtime view taken from St Giles churchyard. The post office appears to be attempting to cater for tourists calling in Ollerton as part of a visit to Sherwood Forest and the Dukeries, for it has a sign reading 'Ye Olde Gift Shoppe'. A little further along the street, the white building is the butcher's shop, owned in the photograph on page 10 by George Essam, and run by this time by C. W. Field. The entrance to the watermill can be seen in almost the last building on the left.

The White Hart Hotel in the centre of the village had once been a coaching inn. It was rebuilt in the 1770s on the site of the original White Hart which was destroyed by fire. From here horse-drawn coaches could be boarded for rides around the Dukeries. Certain innkeepers, who belonged to an association, were issued with keys to allow access to the grounds of the Welbeck, Rufford, Thoresby and Manor estates on designated days each week.

At the beginning of the twentieth century the premises adjoining the White Hart belonged to John Ward, grocer, ham and bacon curer and agent for W. & A. Gilbey Ltd., wine and spirit merchants. On the other side of the road the five boys and the little girl are standing outside William Pinnington's shop. There is a prominent sign advertising Hole's Newark Ales. Newark, some twelve miles distant, was noted for a number of breweries which supplied the surrounding towns and villages. The shop in the far distance belonged to George Charles Cox, one of two saddlers in the village.

Dating from 1909, this photograph was taken looking down Wellow Road with the drapery, milliners and clothing outfitters belonging to William Bowring on the left. There were at least two other shops offering a similar range of goods in the village at this time. A little further down the road is the small shop of C. H. Booth, fruiterer, tobacconist and newsagent. Facing Wellow Road are the premises of W. R. Appleby. His shop is an example of how local traders of this period had to offer a number of goods and services to make a living, for he advertises millinery, mantles, dressmaking, drapery, clothing, house furnishings and boots and shoes for sale.

HIGHSTREET OLLERTON.

This view looks the opposite way to the previous picture and dates from about 25 years later, by which time the first premises up Wellow Road have changed from being a private house to a shop selling ironmongery. The change in the shopping habits of local people in recent years is illustrated by the fact that all the shops on the right of this picture have long since closed and been boarded up.

Wellow Road on the way to the National School. At this time only one side of the street was built up. The only transport in view is a solitary bicycle, although there is evidence in the road of horse-drawn transport having driven by. In the early years of the twentieth century Ollerton would have been totally self-sufficient in shops and craftspeople, and for most people there would have been little need to travel further afield for goods or services.

The photographer was looking from Ollerton towards Wellow when he captured this view of the National School. Lord Manvers of Thoresby Hall was one of the chief supporters of the school, which opened in September 1842. As the only National School within an eight mile radius it had a large catchment area. The building consisted of three rooms heated by a coke-burning stove. In 1908 there were 128 children plus 40 infants on the roll with John Greaves listed as master.

Wellow Road is the main thoroughfare from Ollerton to the village of Wellow and beyond to Newark. The horse and cart has stopped outside the Royal Oak Inn where the licensee was George Henry Scott. A note on the back of this postcard, which was sent from Ollerton to Sheffield on 7 December 1911, indicates that the man with the cart was Bill Askew, who collected refuse locally (see page 25). The white building on the right housed a grocery shop and bakery owned by Walter Germany.

MARKET PLACE OLLERTON.

3847

A similar view to that on page 16 but taken sometime between 1915 and 1925. The Worksop Co-operative Society with John Edward Sleaford as manager has taken over John Ward's grocers shop. Parked close by is the co-op's delivery van. In the foreground, by the draper's shop, is a horse and cart. At this time motor vehicles were increasingly superseding horse-drawn vehicles as the main means of transport for both goods and people.

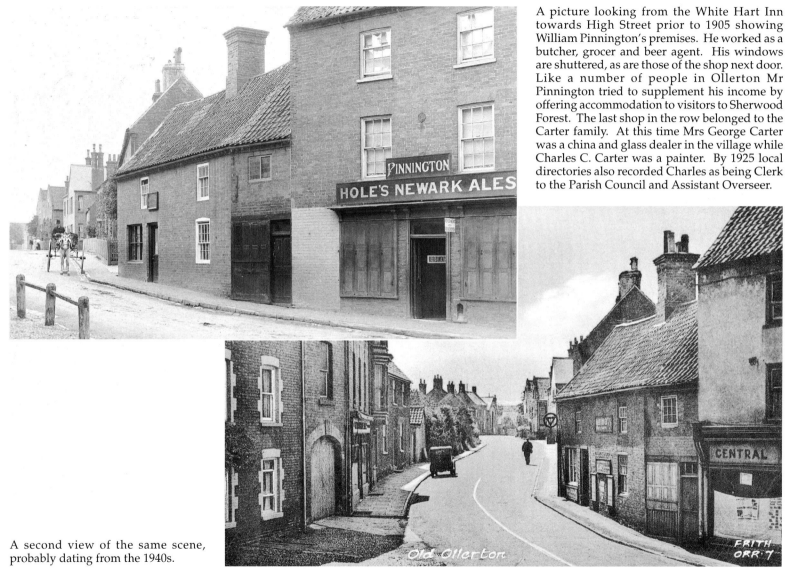

A picture looking from the White Hart Inn towards High Street prior to 1905 showing William Pinnington's premises. He worked as a butcher, grocer and beer agent. His windows are shuttered, as are those of the shop next door. Like a number of people in Ollerton Mr Pinnington tried to supplement his income by offering accommodation to visitors to Sherwood Forest. The last shop in the row belonged to the Carter family. At this time Mrs George Carter was a china and glass dealer in the village while Charles C. Carter was a painter. By 1925 local directories also recorded Charles as being Clerk to the Parish Council and Assistant Overseer.

A second view of the same scene, probably dating from the 1940s.

At the left of this picture taken from the White Hart Inn about 1914 is an example of the old and the new with an early motorcycle, registration number AL 1644, parked outside a saddler's shop. On the right is the newsagents belonging to C. H. Booth. He had moved to these larger premises since 1909 (see page 17), and seemed to specialise in selling Sheffield-based newspapers with adverts for the *Telegraph*, *Star* and *Independent*, all of which were based in that city. The headlines make bizarre reading: 'London Welcomes the Kaiser' and 'Extraordinary Scenes at Midgets' Burial'.

31·10. High St Ollerton. JS.&S.

The larger inns in Ollerton had catered for travellers for hundreds of years, but as the twentieth century progressed more and more smaller establishments also offered services for passing visitors. This section of High Street, photographed in the 1930s, shows three private houses offering bed and breakfast accommodation. The shop on the left also offers cold drinks while one further down advertises 'Teas Provided'. Rose Villa, situated to the right and run by Mrs Gertrude Francis Parkin, particularly welcomes members of the Cyclists Touring Club.

HIGH ST. OLLERTON

Bill Askew's cart makes another appearance, but on this occasion without his horse. The cart is parked outside the Askew family cottage on High Street. Along the road on the same side, beyond the two women in the doorway, is a single-storey shed and pair of entrance gates. It was from here that Mr Waby carried out his business of cabinetmaker and undertaker.

A faded postcard sent from Rufford Cottages, Ollerton on 23 April 1906. The interesting feature is the street light. Records reveal that in 1876 the Revd J. Smith organised a series of concerts to raise funds to provide street lights in Ollerton. These consisted of paraffin lamps fitted on wooden posts, and it is believed that they survived until at least the outbreak of the First World War. Interestingly, none of the other pictures in this book feature street lights in the older part of Ollerton.

As this view along High Street towards St Giles Church illustrates, once away from the bustling centre of Ollerton around the Hop Pole and White Hart, the rest of the village was a sleepy backwater where little changed over many years.

In this picture a traditional rural activity encounters the twentieth century, as a herd of cattle being driven along Station Road hold up the progress of a car.

Views such as this one of Station Road make it difficult not to agree with *Black's Guide to Nottinghamshire* of 1887, which said of Ollerton: 'The town itself is a dull little place presenting nothing of any note'. One significant happening took place in 1905 when early one Sunday there was an earthquake lasting twenty minutes. Perhaps typically of sleepy Ollerton, the press remarked that 'It occasioned more alarm than damage'.

OLLERTON

Another author who was less than complimentary about Ollerton was J. B. Firth, who said: 'the streets are narrow and the houses commonplace'. Despite this criticism, the village is attractively situated on the edge of Sherwood Forest giving easy access to some beautiful countryside. Local grocer W. J. Sterland was particularly intrigued by the wildlife in the forest and wrote two books about his observations including *The Birds of Sherwood Forest*.

This vista towards the end of Station Road has altered considerably in the 90 years since the photograph was taken. The row of terraced houses to the right, where the mother with her yard brush and the girl with her baby are standing, has been demolished, while the area facing them across the road has been developed.

The dwelling on the left with unusual gables and tall chimneys still stands near the end of Station Road today.

Ollerton station was built by the Lancashire, Derbyshire & East Coast Railway Company and opened in 1895. In 1907 ownership transferred to the Great Central Company, which explains the signs advertising trips on the Dominion Line to Canada and the SY *Argonaut* to Norway. The station is decorated with flowers from the grounds of Rufford Abbey in preparation for the arrival of King Edward VII in 1908. The gentleman in the peaked cap was the then stationmaster, Francis Granville Kemp.

Edward VII was extremely keen on the sport of kings, horse racing, and in September each year attended the St Leger meeting at Doncaster. Whilst in the area it was his custom to stay with Lord Savile at Rufford Abbey. He arrived in Nottinghamshire by train, alighting at Ollerton station. On this occasion, in 1906, he presented Mr Kemp the stationmaster with a gold tie pin before being driven the final mile or so to Rufford.

Entry to the Rufford grounds was via these ornate gates, constructed in 1841 and situated on the Nottingham to Doncaster road. Once through them visitors progressed along an avenue flanked by lime trees to the house. Although both the gates and avenue remain they are no longer used.

Rufford Abbey was built by the Cistercians in 1148 and survived as a religious establishment until Henry VIII's dissolution of the monasteries in 1537, when it was granted to the Earls of Shrewsbury. Eventually the Rufford estate passed to the Savile family. Being so large (it extended over 18,000 acres when it was broken up in 1938) and so close to Ollerton, its owners had great influence within and over the village. For instance, in 1793 Sir George Savile was able to alter the course of the road from Nottingham to Ollerton in order to enclose a stretch of land within his estate.

In staying at Rufford Abbey, King Edward VII was following a precedent set by James I and Charles II. The King arrived in September each year accompanied by a number of his friends, and as well as attending the racing at Doncaster there would be excursions to visit local landed families in Nottinghamshire and the surrounding counties. Shooting parties were held at Rufford and his host, Lord Savile, would lay on entertainment. One year the singer Harry Lauder was engaged to perform. After the King's death Lord Savile erected a sundial in the grounds as a memorial to him. In the early years of the twentieth century Rufford had a staff of over 300.

A note on the reverse of this postcard indicates that it shows the erecting of the first telegraph pole in Ollerton in 1909. The location is the bottom of Wellow Road with St Giles churchyard wall just visible to the right. In the background is W. Bowring's drapers shop. Erecting the pole was obviously a labour intensive process that used primitive techniques. Telephone links to the village grew apace in 1924 when the Butterley Company took over Ollerton Hall and needed an efficient communication system to speed up the development of the colliery.

Town Street viewed from close to the Hop Pole. The building to the right belonged to J. Bowring, tailor and woollen draper (William Bowring was in a similar line of business in Wellow Road). The second terrace on the left included Annie Skinn's tobacconists shop (see overleaf).

A picture from *c.*1904 showing Annie Skinn standing in the doorway of her shop. The lady looking in at the window is Mrs Lizzie Anderson with her son Hugh and daughter Ada. (This information comes from the rear of the picture and is a good example of the merits of annotating our photographs for the benefit of future generations!) Annie Skinn was still running her shop twenty years later when the 1925 trade directory was published, but by 1936 ownership had passed to Emily Frances Skinn.

This picture shows the top end of Town Street (furthest from the Hop Pole). The building at the far end, at right angles to the street, is Ollerton Hall. Today Town Street is the main access road to the village.

The original area known as New Ollerton, on Boughton Road, consisted of only a handful of houses on one side of the road. The Wesleyan chapel (illustrated here) was constructed there in 1867. There was also a Primitive Methodist chapel on Station Road but this closed in the 1920s. The Boughton Road chapel was closed in 1974.

BOUGHTON ROAD NEW OLLERTON.

A Plough Inn was established in New Ollerton in the 1840s in a small cottage-type property. For a long time it marked the limit of the village of Ollerton, after which there was open country until the next village of Boughton. This photograph was taken by Sydney Hall of nearby Edwinstowe after the new Plough Inn (right) had been built, and just prior to the construction of the colliery village.

Plough Inn, New Ollerton.

Copyright L.L. Orn. 10

The Plough Inn in 1927. At the time it was not unusual to be able to purchase petrol from a number of different retail outlets including shops and public houses as well as garages. The spacious new Plough Inn was initially used as the meeting point for many of the sporting activities that took place in New Ollerton. When the colliery village was being developed, local Catholics held services there until St Joseph's Catholic church opened in 1929.

NEW OLLERTON COLLIERY.

When Lord Savile sold his coal rights in 1921 exploration for coal began in the Ollerton area. The Butterley Colliery Company commenced tests and the results convinced them of the viability of establishing a colliery. In 1924 the colliery manager moved into Ollerton Hall and arrangements were made to recruit a large workforce. Many families relocated to the village from Scotland and the north-east, and the first coal left Ollerton Colliery on 1 September 1926. In 1968 production exceeded one million tons in a year for the first time, but the decline in the coal industry in the 1990s saw Ollerton close in 1994. The headstocks were demolished in December of that year.

New Ollerton.

The introduction of a new, labour-intensive industry into a predominantly rural area created a need for workers' houses. Concrete huts were built for the men who were sinking the shafts, and other early workers lodged with local families – some it is said having to 'box and cox' with beds so that men coming off shift climbed into beds still warm from miners going to work. These ten houses (one is out of shot to the left) were built by a firm called Coleman opposite the Plough Inn and close to the colliery entrance. They were of quite a high quality and were designed for office workers. In 2001 the houses to the far right were demolished to provide access to a new superstore being built on the former colliery site.

The Butterley Colliery Company's plan was to build 1,000-plus houses using ten different styles to avoid 'monotony of standardisation by types'. The average cost was £420 per house after the Chamberlain subsidy (a government grant to assist house-builders). The properties provided good accommodation for the time, being spacious (866–946 sq. ft) and on good sized plots. The estate had a sophisticated hot water system linked to the exhaust steam that was generated at the pit head, and the ability of the company to offer new houses was an attractive incentive to miners who often relocated hundreds of miles to Ollerton with their families.

Forest Road, New Ollerton.

FRITH. ORR.10.

Central Buildings New Ollerton

The development of a community of a thousand homes required the provision of a variety of ancillary facilities. Forest Road became the main shopping street in the village, and Central Buildings were constructed in a mock-Tudor style at the junction of Forest Road and Sherwood Drive. The cars in the picture would suggest that the photograph dates from the end of the 1940s.

When New Ollerton was built in the 1920s land was a relatively plentiful and cheap commodity, and roads and pavements were made with generous proportions. These shops on Forest Road are typical of the small one-man and family-run businesses which set up in New Ollerton to service the community associated with the colliery.

A 1960s view of Ollerton library on Forest Road. Like many libraries and schools built in Nottinghamshire at this time it used the CLASP system of construction, whereby instead of using bricks and mortar larger prefabricated sections of buildings were assembled.

St. Paulinus Church, New Ollerton.

FRITH.
ORR. 1.

One of the first requirements when forming a new community is to cater for its spiritual needs. Initially a Mission Hall was provided in New Ollerton, then the cemetery chapel on Forest Road, but both quickly became inadequate to meet demand and it was decided to build a new church. The Butterley Company provided £5,000 towards it, while Lord Savile donated the site and £500. Plans were drawn up by Naylor, Sale & Woore of Derby and building began on 13 March 1931. The Bishop of Southwell laid the foundation stone and the work was carried out by Greenwoods of Mansfield. Unfortunately the full plans could not be implemented due to lack of cash, and amid much criticism a tower was not built. The church was named after St Paulinus of York who in the sixth century helped Augustine extend Christianity in England. It opened on 1 October 1932.

In the 1700s a nineteen-acre site, situated between Edwinstowe and Ollerton, was leased by the Revd William Spring from the Welbeck estate. On it he built himself a small country house with landscaped grounds. Around 1778 George Aldrich took over Cockglode House, and in 1832 it was leased to Savile Henry Lumley. Cecil George Savile Foljambe took up residence at Cockglode in 1869, remaining there until 1897. He was an MP and in 1892 was made Baron Hawkesbury. By the beginning of the twentieth century demand for large country houses had declined, and after the Second World War Cockglode was converted into flats. However, this did not prove successful and by 1956 the house had been abandoned. Thoresby Colliery was one of its nearest neighbours and sadly the site of Cockglode House suffered the eventual fate of disappearing under a colliery spoil tip.